MW00388783

For the Teacher

This reproducible study guide to use in conjunction with the book *The Tale of Despereaux* consists of lessons for guided reading. Written in chapter-by-chapter format, the guide contains a synopsis, pre-reading activities, vocabulary and comprehension exercises, as well as extension activities to be used as follow-up to the novel.

In a homogeneous classroom, whole class instruction with one title is appropriate. In a heterogeneous classroom, reading groups should be formed: each group works on a different novel at its reading level. Depending upon the length of time devoted to reading in the classroom, each novel, with its guide and accompanying lessons, may be completed in three to six weeks.

Begin using NOVEL-TIES for reading development by distributing the novel and a folder to each child. Distribute duplicated pages of the study guide for students to place in their folders. After examining the cover and glancing through the book, students can participate in several pre-reading activities. Vocabulary questions should be considered prior to reading a chapter; all other work should be done after the chapter has been read. Comprehension questions can be answered orally or in writing. The classroom teacher should determine the amount of work to be assigned, always keeping in mind that readers must be nurtured and that the ultimate goal is encouraging students' love of reading.

The benefits of using NOVEL-TIES are numerous. Students read good literature in the original, rather than in abridged or edited form. The good reading habits, formed by practice in focusing on interpretive comprehension and literary techniques, will be transferred to the books students read independently. Passive readers become active, avid readers.

Novel-Ties® are printed on recycled paper.

The purchase of this study guide entitles an individual teacher to reproduce pages for use in a classroom. Reproduction for use in an entire school or school system or for commercial use is prohibited. Beyond the classroom use by an individual teacher, reproduction, transmittal or retrieval of this work is prohibited without written permission from the publisher.

Copyright © 2004, 2009 by LEARNING LINKS INC.

SYNOPSIS

The birth of the unlikely mouse hero of this tale is so traumatic for his mother that she names him Despereaux and vows that she will never again bear another litter of mice. From the beginning, Despereaux is a nonconformist in the mouse community. Fascinated with lights, books, and music, he is drawn to an encounter with Princess Pea and her father, King Philip, during which he breaks all conventions of mouse behavior by speaking and then revealing himself to the princess. Smitten with love, he pledges his honor and devotion. For this act, the Mouse Council votes to banish him to the dark castle dungeon, where mouse-eating rats wait to devour any who break the rules of the mouse community. With the red thread of death fastened around his neck by Hovis the threadmaster, Despereaux is ceremoniously escorted by his own brother out of the world of light into the realm of darkness. There he meets Gregory the kindly jailer who, in exchange for stories of knights and fair maidens, keeps Despereaux safe from the rats and promises to find a way to deliver him back up to the light.

One of the rats, Roscuro—short for Chiaroscuro—is a noncomformist like Despereaux. As a result of an early encounter with a match, he, too, is fascinated by light. Despite the counsel of his mentor Botticelli Remorso, who insists that a rat's only pleasure can come from torturing people, Roscuro breaks with convention and pays a visit to the castle banquet hall. Dazzled by the light of the chandelier and the gaiety of a party, Roscuro falls into the queen's soup. The shock of seeing a rat in her soup leads to her untimely death. As a result, the princess consigns Roscuro to the dungeon forever and the king bans soup and all soup-related implements throughout the kingdom. Roscuro, shattered by the princess's condemnation, returns to the dungeon wearing the queen's soup spoon and vowing revenge.

In another part of the kingdom, young Miggery Sow, who lost her mother at a young age and was sold by her father into indentured servitude, is rescued by one of the king's men and brought to the castle in a wagonload of confiscated cooking paraphernalia. Almost deaf from repeated blows to the ears by her cruel master, young Mig fails at one castle job after another until finally she is sent to the "deep downs" with Gregory's lunch tray. There Roscuro overhears her dreams of becoming a princess such as Pea and realizes that she is the perfect instrument of his revenge. With the dimwitted Mig's help, he kidnaps the princess and spirits her away to the dungeon to hold her in perpetual darkness.

Thanks to Gregory's assistance, Despereaux has returned to the world of light. He learns of the princess's fate but is unable to convince the king that he knows where the princess is held; he soon realizes that he must rescue her himself. Armed by Hovis with a needle and supplied with a spool of red thread to lead him through the dungeon's maze, he descends into the depths of his own free will on a quest to rescue Princess Pea.

Aided by the devious Botticelli, Despereaux finally reaches the spot where Roscuro is holding Pea. When Mig realizes that she is being used by Roscuro, she understands that her heart's desire is her mother and not to be a princess. Princess Pea, who has suffered a similar loss, empathizes with Mig and also forgives Roscuro. The book concludes with the characters raised from the dark of the dungeon back into the world of light—all feasting on an enormous kettle of soup.

PRE-READING ACTIVITIES

1. Preview the book by reading the title and the author's name and by looking at the illustration on the cover. Why do you think the author gives this book both a long and a short title? What do you think this book will be about? Will it tell a realistic or a fantastic story? Now glance at some of the illustrations. When and where do you think the story takes place? Have you read other books by this author?

2. *Despereaux* is a French word that means "despair." Make some predictions about a character that has this name. Why might a parent choose this name? What effect might such a name have on an individual?

3. In interviews, the author has revealed that she wrote this novel in response to a request made by a friend's son. When she told him that she didn't usually write stories on command he said, "But this is a story that I know you would tell. It is about an unlikely hero. He has exceptionally large ears." As you read, keep this request in mind so that when you finish, you can comment on whether you think Kate DiCamillo fulfilled Luke Bailey's request.

4. *The Tale of Despereaux* is a Newbery medal-winning book. This award is presented annually to the book that makes the most distinguished contribution to American literature for children or young adults. Think of other award-winning books you have read. What qualities do these books have in common? As you read this novel, decide why it was selected to receive this prestigious award.

5. *The Tale of Despereaux* is classified as a fantasy rather than a fairy tale or science fiction. In your opinion, what important differences exist among these three types of literature? Give examples of books in each category.

6. Light and dark are referred to over and over again in *The Tale of Despereaux*. As you read, notice when light and dark are used and whether they are used in connection with good and bad images, or both.

7. Fantasies usually have a hero and a villain as central characters. A hero is a courageous character who is admired for brave deeds and noble qualities. This person is regarded as a model or an ideal. A villain is a character who is devoted to wickedness and evil. List some heroes and villains whom you know from stories, films, or television programs. Create a web around each character in which you record words that describe his or her personality and character. As you read the book, notice the heroes and villains. Do they possess the same character traits that you recorded in your character webs? What differences do you notice?

8. A novel's theme is its central idea or message. The struggle against conformity and consequences of rebellion against the rules is an important theme in this novel. In a small group, discuss what conformity means and what happens when people rebel against society's established rules.

CHAPTERS 1 – 8

Vocabulary: Draw a line from each word on the left to its definition on the right. Then use the numbered words to fill in the blanks in the sentences below.

1. rodents
2. siblings
3. conform
4. indulge
5. scurry
6. ordeal

a. behave like others
b. move hurriedly
c. mammals that gnaw
d. difficult experience
e. brothers and sisters
f. yield to

. . . .

1. Mice, rats, squirrels, and porcupines are all common forms of _____.

2. Climbing the steep mountain on a hot summer day was a terrible _____.

3. If I _____ in rich food before bedtime, I know I will have bad dreams.

4. As soon as we turned on the light, we heard the mice _____ back into their hole.

5. Soldiers must dress in the same way and _____ to the same set of rules.

6. My parents, _____, and I always enjoy our summer family vacation at the beach.

> Read to find out how Despereaux Tilling got his name.

Questions:

1. Why did the mother mouse name her last baby Despereaux?

2. Why did Despereaux's siblings and other relatives view him as such a disappointment?

3. What amazing discovery did Despereaux make when Merlot took him into the castle library?

4. Why did Lester call a special meeting of the Mouse Council?

5. How did Despereaux break two of the most basic and ancient of all mouse rules? Why did he break each rule?

6. Why did King Philip object so strenuously to Princess Pea's behavior?

Chapters 1 – 8 (cont.)

Questions for Discussion:

1. Do you think Antoinette and Lester Tilling behaved toward their son in an appropriate way?

2. What do you think the author meant when she said, "Reader, you must know that an interesting fate (sometimes involving rats, sometimes not) awaits almost everyone, mouse or man, who does not confirm"? Do you agree with this statement?

3. What do you think Despereaux meant in his parting words to Princess Pea at the conclusion of Chapter Seven? What significance do you think these words might have?

4. Do you agree that Lester committed an act of perfidy? Under what circumstances, if any, should a parent be willing to sacrifice a child whose behavior is believed to endanger the safety of the community?

Literary Devices:

I. *Point of View*—Point of view in a book of fiction refers to the person telling the story. It could be one of the characters or it could be the author narrating the story. Who is telling this story?

How does the voice telling this story help you understand things that you might have missed?

_____

_____

Why do you think the author of this story "talks" to the reader directly?

_____

_____

II. *Irony*—Irony refers to a situation that is the opposite of what is expected. Considering the description of Despereaux at the beginning of the book, what is ironic about his falling in love with a beautiful princess?

_____

_____

Chapters 1 – 8 (cont.)

III. *Simile*—A simile is a figure of speech in which two unlike objects are compared using the words "like" or "as." For example:

"Oh," he said, "it [music] sounds like heaven. It smells like honey."

What is music compared to in this simile?

_____

How do these similes help you understand Despereaux's feelings about music?

_____

_____

IV. *Personification*—Personification is a figure of speech in which an author grants life-like qualities to a nonhuman object. For example:

The April sun, weak but determined, shone through a castle window and from there squeezed itself through a small hole in the wall and placed one golden finger on the little mouse.

What is being personified?

_____

Why is this better than saying, "The sun shone on the mouse"?

_____

_____

Internet Activity:

Learn more about castles by visiting these sites on the Internet:
http://www.castlesontheweb.com
http://42explore.com/castle.htm.
Share the information by drawing a diagram, building a model, or writing a report.

Writing Activity:

Despereaux's love for music is such a powerful force that he loses his head and acts against his mouse instincts to keep himself hidden from humans. Write about a time when you felt swept away by music. Tell what you were listening to and how this music made you feel.

Chapters 1 – 8 (cont.)

Literary Element: Characterization

Fill in the chart below with information about the major characters you have met in the first eight chapters. Add to the chart as you meet other important characters in the book.

Character	Information
Despereaux	
Furlough	
Princess Pea	
King Philip	

CHAPTERS 9 – 15

Vocabulary: Analogies are equations in which the first pair of words has the same relationship as the second pair of words. For example: BOOKS are to LIBRARY as CROCKERY is to CUPBOARD. Both words name objects and the places where they are found. Choose the best word to complete each analogy. Circle the letter of the word you choose.

1. TELLING is to _____ as CRYING is to SOBBING.

    a. calling   b. inviting   c. commanding   d. sensing

2. GASP is to LUNGS as _____ is to EYES.

    a. gaze   b. sniff   c. breathe   d. exhale

3. DEFY is to REFUSE as DISOWN is to _____.

    a. bellow   b. inherit   c. pronounce   d. renounce

4. VILLAIN is to PERFIDY as KNIGHT is to _____.

    a. cowardice   b. devotion   c. triumph   d. defiance

5. DECADES are to CENTURIES as EONS are to _____.

    a. calendar   b. months   c. eternities   d. timelines

> Read to find out what happened when Despereaux went before the Mouse Council.

Questions:

1. How did Despereaux react when Furlough told him that he had been called by the Mouse Council?

2. What egregious acts did the Mouse Council accuse Despereaux of committing? What defense did he offer?

3. Why did Despereaux refuse to renounce his actions? How did the mouse community react to his refusal to repent?

4. What role did the threadmaster play in Despereaux's fate? How did his treatment of Despereaux differ from that of the other mice?

5. Why was the word *perfidy* in Despereaux's mind as he was led to the dungeon?

6. How did Despereaux comfort himself when he was cast into the dungeon?

7. Why did Gregory offer to save Despereaux's life?

Chapters 9 – 15 (cont.)

Questions for Discussion:

1. Why do you think Despereaux failed to realize the seriousness of the situation when Furlough confronted him? How did Furlough use Despereaux's response to justify his own actions?

2. Why do you think the mouse community felt threatened by Despereaux? Would a human with traits like those of Despereaux threaten people in the real world? In your opinion, did Despereaux receive a fair trial?

3. How do you think the threadmaster knew about fairy tales and courtly love?

4. What do you think the author meant when she said that "farewell" is a word that in any language is full of sorrow?

5. What do you think Gregory meant when he said, "stories are light"?

Literary Devices:

I. *Repetition*—Repetition is the repeated use of any element of language, such as a word, phrase, sound, or rhythmic pattern. For example:

> Perfidy. Pea. Perfidy Pea. These were the words that pinwheeled through Despereaux's mind as his body descended into darkness.

Why does the author repeat the words *perfidy* and *Pea* at this point in the story?

_____

_____

Repetition of a consonant sound is called *alliteration*. In addition to the sound of the letter *p*, what other example of alliteration can you find in the example above?

_____

II. *Cliffhanger*—A cliffhanger in literature is a device borrowed from silent, serialized films in which an episode ends at a moment of suspense. In a book, it usually appears at the end of a chapter to encourage the reader to continue on in the book.

What is the cliffhanger at the end of Chapter Fourteen?

_____

Chapters 9 – 15 (cont.)

III. *Foreshadowing*—Foreshadowing is the use of clues by the author to prepare the reader for future developments in the plot. Explain what you think this exchange between Despereaux and Gregory might foreshadow:

> "Look on that, mouse," said Gregory. "That is a monument to the foolishness of love."
>
> "What is it?" asked Despereaux. He stared at the great tower that reached up, up, up into the blackness.
>
> "What it looks like. Spoons, Bowls, Kettles. All of them gathered here as hard evidence of the pain of loving a living thing. The king loved the queen and the queen died; this monstrosity, this junk heap is the result of love."

\
\

IV. *Irony*—Explain the irony in this observation of Gregory's:

> "You are talking to Gregory the jailer, who, in the richest of ironies, is nothing but a prisoner here himself."

\
\

Language Study:

Many mice in this novel have French names and use French words. When Despereaux's mother first set eyes on him, she exclaims, *"Mon Dieu!,"* which is French for "my goodness!" She also uses French words to name her children. Find out the meaning and pronunciation of each of the following words:

Word	Pronunciation	Meaning
merlot		
oui		
adieu		

Chapters 9 – 15 (cont.)

Social Studies Connection: Courtly Love and Chivalry

While securing the loop of red thread around Despereaux's neck, the threadmaster describes Despereaux's love for the princess as "courtly love, a love that is based on bravery and courtesy and honor and devotion." In other words, a love that is admirable, virtuous, and noble. Courtly love of knights towards fair maidens is associated with the code of chivalry in the Middle Ages. Use the Internet or reference materials to find out more information about courtly love. Then write a brief report answering these questions:

- How does courtly love differ from romantic love?

- What are some characteristics of courtly love?

- Based on this information, did Despereaux exhibit feelings of courtly love towards Princess Pea?

Writing Activities:

1. When cast into the dungeon, Despereaux wills himself to be brave by thinking of the words of the threadmaster and then by telling himself a story. Think of a time when you willed yourself to be brave. Describe the incident and tell whether you managed to find the courage you needed.

2. In her description of the castle dungeon, the author incorporates details that focus on how it smells and feels as well as how it looks. Write a description of a real or imaginary place that you would find terrifying. Include sensory details to help the reader imagine the scene.

CHAPTERS 16 – 18

Vocabulary: Synonyms are words with similar meanings. Draw a line from each word in column A to its synonym in column B. Then use the words in Column A to fill in the blanks in the sentences below.

	A		B
1.	domain	a.	shrewd
2.	despicable	b.	compulsion
3.	astute	c.	comfort
4.	obsession	d.	excessive
5.	inordinate	e.	realm
6.	solace	f.	hateful

. . . .

1. As a (n) _____ poker player, I expected to win the card game quickly and easily.

2. A room cluttered from floor to ceiling is the result of my _____ with comic books.

3. In the eyes of the enemy, the prisoners were _____ creatures, not even worthy of notice.

4. Despite her sadness, Jane was able to find some _____ and relief by spending many hours a day in her garden caring for her plants.

5. From a very early age, Linda showed a (n) _____ interest in all music; listening to it on the radio for at least four hours a day.

6. In many old castles, mice and people inhabit the upper floors, while the dungeon is the _____ of rats.

> Read to find out who Despereaux met in the dungeon.

Questions:

1. What is the meaning of the word *chiaroscuro*? In what ways did Chiaroscuro, or Roscuro for short, live up to his name?

2. How did Roscuro and Botticelli differ in their views on the meaning of life? What was Botticelli's advice on how Roscuro could make his life meaningful?

3. Why was Botticelli so sure that Roscuro would soon have a prisoner to torture?

Chapters 16 – 18 (cont.)

4. How did Roscuro apply Botticelli's advice on how to make his life meaningful? What was the result?

5. Why wasn't Roscuro shocked by the man's confession?

Questions for Discussion:

1. Why do you think Chiaroscuro was usually called Roscuro rather than by his full name? What significance did this have?

2. Why do you think Botticelli was so disapproving of Roscuro's inordinate interest in light? Where else in the story have you seen this type of disapproval?

3. Do you agree that torture can consist of emotional pain as well as physical pain? Which type of pain do you think is harder to bear?

4. What do you think Gregory really meant when he told the prisoner that "you'll need every last bit of warmth down here"?

Literary Devices:

I. *Allusion*—An allusion is a reference in literature to a familiar person, place, object, event, or saying. One of the characters in this novel is named after Botticelli—a famous Italian artist. Botticelli was known for his use of chiaroscuro, which as you know is the arrangement of light and dark in a painting. Look up this painter in an encyclopedia or on the Internet to help you answer these questions:

• What was the mood or tone of most of Botticelli's work?

_____

_____

• Why do you think the author alluded to him?

_____

_____

In another allusion, when Roscuro is forced to admit that he is a rat, he concludes with the words "World without end. Amen." This is the ending to a well-known Christian prayer, called *The Apostle's Creed*. In what way is Roscuro's statement like a creed, or statement of belief?

_____

_____

Chapters 16 – 18 (cont.)

II. *Flashback*—A flashback interrupts the chronological sequence of events in a novel to relate something that happened at an earlier time. What flashback occurs in this book?

_____

III. *Elevated Language*—Elevated language is formal, dignified language. It can be used to give dignity to a hero, to reveal a self-important character, or for humor. For example:

> "I am," said Roscuro, "exactly that. A rat. Allow me to congratulate you on your very astute powers of observation."

What purpose does Roscuro's elevated language serve in this example?

_____

_____

Literary Elements: Characterization

Roscuro and Despereaux are as different as night and day, but they also share several traits in common. Compare these two characters in the Venn diagram below. Record the ways that the two characters differ in the outer portions of the circles. Then jot down characteristics that they have in common in the overlapping part of the circles.

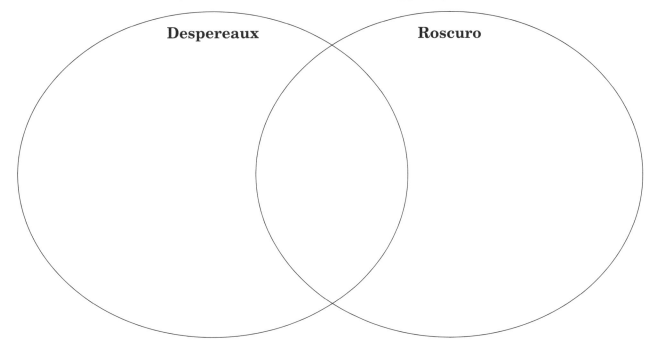

Chapters 16 – 18 (cont.)

Art Connection:

An artist uses chiaroscuro in order to make a flat, two-dimensional art work look like a three-dimensional solid form. It does this by using highlights and shadows. Here is an example of a drawing of a ball that uses chiaroscuro to make a circle appear as a sphere.

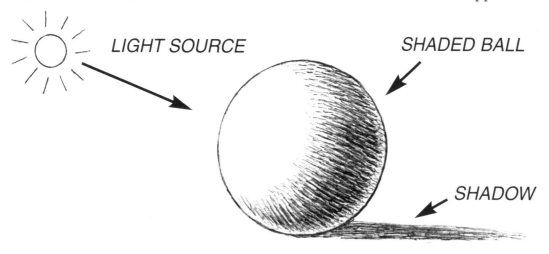

Try drawing a three-dimensional shape using chiaroscuro. Use your pencil to create different shades of light and dark gray. Use a black pen to show the shadow cast by the object.

Writing Activity:

Imagine you are a prisoner and write a journal entry describing your thoughts and feelings on the day you were sent to the dungeon.

CHAPTERS 19 – 23

Vocabulary: Antonyms are words with opposite meanings. Draw a line from each word in column A to its antonym in column B. Then use the words in column A to fill in the blanks in the sentences below.

A	B
1. ornate	a. pleasant
2. flung	b. limited
3. unsavory	c. inconsequential
4. dire	d. plain
5. capacious	e. obscure
6. glaring	f. clutched

. . . .

1. Whenever the guards _____ open the doors to the dungeon, the captives rushed to stand in the light.

2. The moth's obsession with the street light had unintended and _____ consequences that threatened to put it in great danger.

3. The _____ kettle held gallons and gallons of savory soup.

4. The king's _____ crown was studded with jewels of all shapes and sizes.

5. The _____ eyes of the boxers stared at each other with anger and hostility.

6. Even a cockroach's mother would have to agree with the opinion that a roach is by definition a(n) _____ and unattractive insect.

> Read to find out what happened when Roscuro paid a visit upstairs.

Questions:

1. Why was Roscuro enchanted by the scene he witnessed in the banquet hall?

2. What sudden revelation struck Roscuro as he hung from the chandelier? What disastrous consequences resulted from this action?

3. Why did Roscuro look back? Why did this backward glance have such great impact on him?

Chapters 19 – 23 (cont.)

4. How did Roscuro attempt to mend his broken heart?

5. How did King Philip respond to the queen's death? Why weren't his edicts totally successful?

6. Why had so many kettles, bowls, and spoons been heaped in the dungeon?

Questions for Discussion:

1. Do you think Roscuro was to blame for the queen's death?

2. Do you agree that all living things have a heart, and the heart of any living thing can be broken? What implications might this have if everyone believed it?

3. Do you think that every action, no matter how small, has a consequence?

4. Under what circumstances, if any, should a ruler be forgiven for making ridiculous laws? Do you think that King Philip should be forgiven?

Literary Devices:

I. *Understatement*—An understatement is a literary device that tends to make something less important or less dramatic than it really is. For example:

> Roscuro climbed out of the bowl of soup. He felt that under the circumstances, it would be best if he left.

Why would this be termed an understatement?

_____

_____

II. *Symbolism*—A symbol in literature is an object, a person, or an event that represents an idea or set of ideas. What do you think the soupspoon and the cape made out of a scrap of the red tablecloth each symbolize?

_____

_____

_____

Chapters 19 – 23 (cont.)

III. *Cliffhanger*—What is the cliffhanger at the end of Chapter Twenty-three?

_____

_____

Graphic Organizer:

On a separate sheet of paper, create a flowchart, such as the one below, using boxes and arrows to record the series of consequences that stemmed from young Roscuro's gnawing on Gregory the jailer's rope. For example:

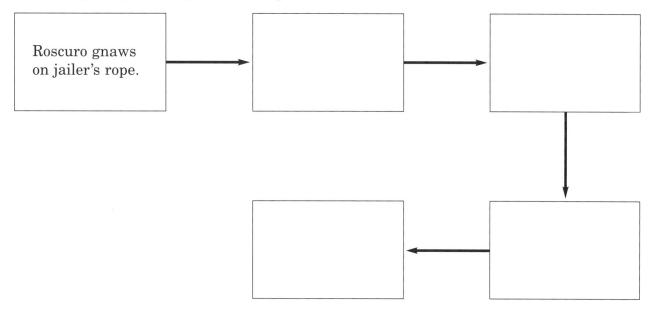

Writing Activities:

1. When a person dies, friends of the family often send a condolence card and write a note. Pretend that you are a friend of Princess Pea. Write her a note in which you express your sympathy for the death of her mother, the Queen.

2. Roscuro was dazzled when he observed the banquet hall. Write about a real or imagined time when you were dazzled by something or a place that you had never seen before.

CHAPTERS 24 – 29

Vocabulary: Choose a word from the Word Box to replace the underlined word or phrase in each of the sentences below. Write the word you choose on the line below the sentence.

WORD BOX		
bold	grim	scrupulously
clout	innumerable	vicious

1. Glenn felt as if he were trapped in a <u>cruel</u> circle—the more he practiced his clarinet, the worse his playing became.

   _____

2. When Anne looked out the window, she saw <u>countless</u> stars winking and twinkling in the night sky.

   _____

3. The jailer picked up a stick and threatened to give the prisoner a sharp <u>blow</u> if he ever tried to escape again.

   _____

4. The few men who managed to return from the expedition told <u>ghastly</u> stories about conditions in the swamp.

   _____

5. Rosanna was <u>painstakingly</u> careful to always have clean hands before looking at the beautiful book of fairy tales that her grandmother had given her.

   _____

6. The king found the jester's <u>impudent</u> behavior to be more annoying than amusing.

   _____

> Read to find out how Miggery Sow came to be on a wagon of soup kettles making its way to the castle.

Chapters 24 – 29 (cont.)

Questions:

1. How was Mig related to one of the characters you have already met in the story?

2. How was Mig trapped in a vicious circle?

3. How did light come into Mig's life? What hopes did it spark?

4. How did Mig finally escape from her cruel owner?

5. Why was Mig allowed to visit Princess Pea? How did Pea react to Mig's curtsy and the information Mig shared about her life and her hopes? What did this reveal about Pea?

6. What has happened to the spools of red thread that Princess Pea complained about using?

7. Why did Louise laugh at Mig?

Questions for Discussion:

1. Who do you think had the crueler father, Despereaux or Miggery Sow?

2. What reaction did you have when you read about Mig's fate? Could a situation such as this ever happen in real life?

3. Do you think that hope is a good thing when things seem absolutely hopeless? And which is worse—false hope or hopelessness?

Literary Device: Flashback

What is the purpose of the flashback that begins in Chapter Twenty-four?

_____

_____

_____

Writing Activity

Write about something that you hope for. Explain why this is your hope and whether you think your wish will ever be fulfilled.

Chapters 24 – 29 (cont.)

Art/Social Studies Connection:

A tapestry is a heavy woven fabric decorated with designs or pictures that often show scenes from history or mythology. During the Middle Ages, tapestries were hung on castle walls as decoration and to keep out freezing drafts. In the space below, create a paper tapestry illustrating scenes from your life and the people you care about. Within the border, use a decorative motif or draw pictures of your home and community.

CHAPTERS 30 – 33

Vocabulary: Read each group of words. Choose the one word that does not belong with the others and cross it out. On the lines below the words, tell how the rest of the words are alike.

1. ominous   frightening   oozing   disturbing

   These words are alike because they all _____

2. candle   spoons   bowls   kettles

   These words are alike because they all _____

3. lady-in-waiting   duchess   seamstress   chambermaid

   These words are alike because they all _____

4. cloak   gown   frock   napkin

   These words are alike because they all _____

5. intently   enthusiastically   passionately   diabolically

   These words are alike because they all _____

6. aspiration   triumph   glory   victory

   These words are alike because they all _____

> Read to find out what happens when Mig is sent down to the dungeon.

Questions:

1. Why did Mig have difficulty performing any job well? What consequences resulted from this failure?

2. Why wasn't Mig bothered by the stench of the dungeon? How did she give herself courage to go into the deep downs?

3. Why was Roscuro delighted when he overheard Mig's conversation with Gregory?

4. How did Gregory help Despereaux?

5. Why was Mig's conversation with Roscuro different from her conversation with everyone else? How did Roscuro win her confidence?

Chapters 30 – 33 (cont.)

Questions for Discussion:

1. Do you think Roscuro will take advantage of Mig as did her father and the man he sold her to?

2. How do you think Mig might help Roscuro get his revenge against Princess Pea for scorning him?

3. What do you think Despereaux will do once he is out of the dungeon?

Literacy Device: Idioms

An idiom is an expression that is understood even though the words do not mean exactly what they say. For example: *raining cats and dogs* means that it is raining very hard. What does the underlined idiom in the following sentence really mean?

"And, too, she [Mig] was <u>not the sharpest knife in the drawer</u>."

Science Connection:

As you learned in Chapter Thirty-one, repeated blows to Mig's nose damaged her olfactory senses. Your olfactory organs have to do with your sense of smell. Try this experiment to see how your senses of taste and smell work together when you eat food.

1. With a partner, prepare small cubes of potato and onion and place them on paper towels.

2. Blindfold your partner. Using a toothpick, give your partner a cube of potato or a cube of onion and ask him or her to identify it. Repeat with the other food. Have your partner identify each taste.

3. Then repeat the taste test, but this time, ask your partner to pinch his or her nostrils closed while tasting the foods. What happens when you ask your partner to identify the foods?

4. After both of you have tried this experiment, discuss your observations. What conclusions can you reach about the ways in which your sense of smell and sense of taste work together? How might this help explain why people often lose their appetites when they have a bad cold?

Writing Activity:

Write a dialogue between Mig and Cook in which she scolds Mig for her inability to perform the simplest of domestic tasks. Then ask a friend to help you perform the dialogue as Readers Theater.

CHAPTERS 34 – 39

Vocabulary: Use the context to help you figure out the meaning of the underlined word in each of the following sentences. Then compare your definitions with those you find in a dictionary.

1. Droplets of water ran down the dank dungeon walls and formed a <u>slick</u> film over the dungeon's floor.

    Your definition: _____

    Dictionary definition: _____

2. The puppy hid in the corner when anyone raised a hand in an <u>ominous</u> gesture.

    Your definition: _____

    Dictionary definition: _____

3. The soldiers were on a <u>covert</u> mission to blow up a bridge deep in enemy territory.

    Your definition: _____

    Dictionary definition: _____

4. Louise believed it was a fitting <u>comeuppance</u> when Brad didn't get a part in the play after he boasted that he was the only one handsome enough to play the part of Romeo.

    Your definition: _____

    Dictionary definition: _____

5. Sunlight shining through stained glass <u>dappled</u> the floor of the library with pools of colored light.

    Your definition: _____

    Dictionary definition: _____

6. The winner showed she was a kind and <u>empathetic</u> person because she could sympathize with the other runners' feeling of sadness when they lost the race.

    Your definition: _____

    Dictionary definition: _____

Read to find out what happens when Roscuro began to put his diabolical plan into action.

Chapters 34 – 39 (cont.)

Questions:

1. How did Mig show her kindness toward Despereaux?

2. Why did Despereaux weep for joy and from pain once he was free?

3. What "divine comeuppance" did Roscuro plan for Princess Pea? How did the rat's real plan differ from the one he presented to Mig?

4. Why did Princess Pea react with hidden rage when she recognized Roscuro?

5. Why were Cook and Louise upset?

Questions for Discussion:

1. Do you think Mig deserved Princess Pea's feelings of empathy? Is she aware of the evil that exists in carrying out her wishes?

2. In your opinion, are there ever any times when revenge is justified?

3. What do you think will happen when Despereaux finds the king?

Literary Devices:

I. *Sarcasm*—Sarcasm is the use of sharp, taunting, or scornful remarks intended to hurt or make fun of someone or something. What does Cook really mean by this comment when Mig announces she is back from the deep downs.

"Ah, lovely," said Cook. "And ain't we all relieved."

II. *Symbolism*—What do you think soup symbolizes in Pea's dream?

What do you think soup symbolizes in Cook's conversation with Louise?

Writing Activity:

Write a court announcement addressed to the people of his kingdom in which the king reveals that the Princess is missing. Describe all he knows about her disappearance and tell what he thinks has happened to her.

CHAPTERS 40 – 46

Vocabulary: Use the words in the Word Box and the clues below to complete the crossword puzzle.

WORD BOX
audible
despair
detect
devious
emphatic
incredible
inspiring
maze
quest
repent
uttered

Across
1. having a stimulating effect
4. loud enough to be heard
7. spoken with great emphasis
8. attempting to deceive
9. lack of all hope
11. feel sorry for something one has done

Down
2. astonishing or amazing
3. search for something of great worth
5. said aloud
6. complicated arrangement of paths through which it is difficult to find the way
10. notice the presence of something

Read to find out what happened when Despereaux found the king.

Questions:

1. Why were the members of the Mice Council terrified when Despereaux appeared before them?
2. Why did Despereaux's father cry after speaking to his son?
3. Why didn't the king believe Despereaux? What effect did this encounter have on the mouse?

Chapters 40 – 46 (cont.)

4. How did the threadmaster help Despereaux on his quest? Why did he call Despereaux "a mouse among mice"?

5. Why did Cook make a bargain with Despereaux? How did she help Despereaux on his quest?

6. How did Despereaux feel as he stood at the top of the dungeon stairs? How did he overcome his reluctance to go down into the darkness again?

Questions for Discussion:

1. Do you agree that forgiveness is as important to the forgiver as to the one who is forgiven? Should Despereaux have granted his father forgiveness?

2. How might the story have changed if the king had believed that Despereaux was telling the truth?

3. Do you agree with the threadmaster that in most cases, it is up to each individual to do the really disagreeable jobs? Think of several examples from your own life to illustrate your opinion.

4. Do you think that Cook should be punished for disobeying the king's law?

Literary Devices:

I. *Symbolism*—What does Cook's soup symbolize?

_____

_____

II. *Cliffhanger*—What is the cliffhanger at the end of Chapter Forty-six?

_____

III. *Personification*—What is being personified in this passage?

> And then the thread, eager, perhaps, to begin its honorable task of aiding in the saving of a princess, leapt forward and away from the mouse and went down the dungeon stairs ahead of him, without him.

_____

Why is this better than saying, "The spool of red thread rolled down the dungeon stairs ahead of the mouse"?

_____

Chapters 40 – 46 (cont.)

Math Connection:

The author says that Despereaux pushed a spool of thread that weighed almost as much as he. Use a bathroom scale to determine how much a classroom dictionary weighs. About how many dictionaries would equal your weight?

- 1 dictionary   = _____ pounds _____ ounces

- ____ dictionaries = _____ pounds
  your weight

Writing Activity:

Imagine that you are Despereaux and you are leaving a note for the king as you begin your quest for the Princess Pea.

CHAPTERS 47 – CODA

Vocabulary: Use one word from the Word Box to replace the underlined word or phrase in each of the following sentences. Write the word you choose on the line below the sentence.

WORD BOX		
atone	contemplate	thwarted
consigned	dire	vengeful

1. The climber realized that he was in a <u>serious</u> situation when an unexpected blizzard blew up just as he reached the top of the mountain.

   _____

2. Our plan to attach the trailer to the back of the car was <u>unsuccessful</u> when the hitch snapped in two.

   _____

3. The <u>cruel</u> dictator sentenced those who opposed his political views to life imprisonment.

   _____

4. In order to <u>ask forgiveness</u> for his misbehavior, Nicco promised to mow the lawn for a year without being asked.

   _____

5. Before she got married, Aunt Eleanor <u>delivered</u> all of her old love letters to the recycling bin.

   _____

6. It is hard for me to <u>think about</u> the fun of skiing since I have always lived far from a snowy mountain.

   _____

Read to find out what happened when Despereaux met the princess again.

Questions:

1. Why did Botticelli offer to lead Despereaux to the princess?
2. What terrible truths did Roscuro offer Mig and Pea?
3. Why did Mig refuse to chain up the princess?
4. Why did Roscuro plead with Despereaux to kill him? Why did Pea intervene?
5. What happiness did each story character find at the end of the story?

Chapters 47 – Coda (cont.)

Questions for Discussion:

1. Were you surprised by Pea's ability to forgive Roscuro? How might the story ending have changed if she had not made this decision?

2. What do you think the author meant when she said that Roscuro never really belonged in either the darkness of the dungeon or the light of the upstairs?

3. How did the author prepare her readers for a sequel to *The Tale of Despereaux*?

Literary Device: Repetition

What do you notice about the meaning of words "Zero", "Zip", "Nada," and "Goose Eggs"?

_____

Why do you think the author used four words in succession that all have the same meaning?

_____

_____

Literary Elements:

I. *Climax*—The climax of a novel is the moment of greatest interest or excitement. It is the point at which interest in the outcome is the highest. What do you think is the climax of *The Tale of Despereaux*?

_____

_____

What makes this climax exciting and satisfying?

_____

_____

II. *Themes*—One theme, or central message, of *The Tale of Despereaux* is the struggle between light (good) and evil (dark). Another important theme is that forgiving of others can lead to one's own happiness. Using Despereaux, Princess Pea, Roscuro, and Miggery Sow, tell how the events in this novel illustrate both themes.

Writing Activity:

The author hints that Despereaux and the princess shared many wonderful adventures together over the years. Write a short story describing one of these adventures. If possible, involve other major story characters in the plot line. Try to use several literary devices that you explored when reading *The Tale of Despereaux*. Share your finished story with a small group or the rest of the class.

CLOZE ACTIVITY

The following passage is taken from Chapter 46 of the book. Read the entire passage before filling in the blanks. Then reread the passage and fill in each blank with a word that makes sense. Finally, you may compare your words with those of the author.

He [Despereaux] had forgotten how dark the dark of the dungeon could be. And he had forgotten, too, its _____ [1] smell, the stench of rats, the odor _____ [2] suffering.

But his heart was full of _____ [3] for the princess and his stomach was _____ [4] of Cook's soup and Despereaux felt brave _____ [5] strong. And so he began, immediately and _____ [6] despair the hard work of maneuvering the _____ [7] of thread down the narrow dungeon steps.

_____ [8] down, down went Despereaux Tilling and the spool _____ [9] thread. Slowly, oh so slowly, they went. _____ [10] the passage was dark, dark, dark.

"I _____ [11] tell myself a story," said Despereaux. "I _____ [12] make some light. Let's see. It will _____ [13] this way. Once upon a time. Yes. _____ [14] upon a time, there was a mouse _____ [15] was very, very small. Exceptionally small. And _____ [16] was a beautiful human princess whose name _____ [17] Pea. And it so happened that this _____ [18] was the one who was selected by _____ [19] to serve the princess, to honor her, _____ [20] to save her from the darkness of _____ [21] terrible dungeon."

This story cheered up Despereaux _____ [22]. His eyes became accustomed to the gloom, _____ [23] he moved down the stairs more quickly, _____ [24] surely, whispering to himself the tale of _____ [25] devious rat and a fat serving girl _____ [26] a beautiful princess and a brave mouse _____ [27] some soup and a spool of red _____ [28]. It was a story, in fact, very similar to the one you are reading right now, and the telling of it gave Despereaux strength.

POST-READING ACTIVITIES

1. Return to title page of the book and reread the whole title, paying particular attention to the subtitle. What importance do some soup and a spool of thread have in the book? What might be another appropriate title for this novel?

2. Kate DiCamillo wrote this novel at the request of a young friend who wanted to read a story about an unlikely hero with exceptionally large ears. In your opinion, does *The Tale of Despereaux* meet this criterion? What evidence would you offer to prove that Despereaux is a heroic character?

3. In "Book the First," Despereaux discovers the joys of reading and the light that comes from a story well told. His ability as a storyteller brings light to Gregory and saves him from a terrible fate in the dungeon. In both the novel's foreword and its coda, the author describes stories as precious light that can help save us from the darkness of the world. In what way are stories light? What light did you discover by reading *The Tale of Despereaux*?

4. *The Tale of Despereaux* was the winner of the Newbery Award in 2004. Write a letter to the judges of this competition telling whether you feel the novel deserved this prestigious award. Support your answer by comparing it to other award-winning books that you have read and by quoting from passages found in the book.

5. The conflict between good and evil is at the heart of *The Tale of Despereaux*. What story characters are on the side of good? What characters are on the side of evil? Are there any characters that are transformed by their exposure to light? What do you think Botticelli Remorso would say if Despereaux accused him of being evil? Is there any hope of his transformation?

6. *The Tale of Despereaux* recounts important events in the lives of four main characters— Despereaux, Princess Pea, Roscuro, and Mig. Use four colored pencils to create four timelines showing the events in each character's life. Then cut out and paste the timelines to put the overlapping events on top of each other. Use the timelines to talk about how the author uses the literary device of flashbacks to weave the four lives together so that they all converge at the climax of the story.

7. What is the role of the threadmaster in this story? What makes him so different from the other mice? Why do you think the author ends the story with the threadmaster's pronouncement, "Just so"?

8. **Readers Theater:** Work with a partner or in a small group to present a chapter that has a lot of dialogue. As you practice, pay attention to phrasing and expression; you may also wish to make a tape recording to help assess your oral reading. When you are ready, share your dramatic reading with the class.

Post-Reading Activities (cont.)

9. In an interview posted on the KidsReads.com website, Kate DiCamillo said, "Every well-written book is a light for me. When you write, you use other writers and their books as guides in the wilderness. I am deeply appreciative of all those writers who work hard to tell their stories right and true, thereby showing me the way to tell my own stories." What did you learn about writing a story from reading *The Tale of Despereaux*? Do you think Kate DiCamillo works hard to tell her story right and true? How might this book serve as a model for other writers?

10. Decide on a creative way that you would like to share *The Tale of Despereaux* with others. You might write up an interview with one of the characters. You could also make a story quilt or tapestry, design a book cover, create an advertisement, dramatize a chapter with puppets, or make a diorama showing your favorite scene from the book. Choose one of these ideas or come up with your own. Then present your finished project to others who might enjoy reading this book.

11. **Literature Circle:** Have a literature circle discussion in which you tell your personal reactions to *The Tale of Despereaux*. Here are some questions and sentence starters to help your literature circle begin a discussion.

    * Do you think the animal characters in this story are like people in any ways?

    * Which character is most like you?

    * Who else would you like to have read this novel? Why?

    * What questions would you like to ask the author about this novel?

    * I wonder . . .

    * I didn't understand . . .

    * It was not fair when . . .

    * It was exciting when . . .

    * It was funny when . . .

    * I learned that . . .

SUGGESTIONS FOR FURTHER READING

* Aiken, Joan. *Black Hearts in Battersea*. Houghton Mifflin.

   _____. *The Wolves of Willoughby Chase*. Random House.

   Avi. *City of Light, City of Dark: A Comic-Book Novel*. Scholastic.

* Cooper, Susan. *The Dark is Rising*. Simon & Schuster.

* Cleary, Beverly. *The Mouse and the Motorcycle*. HarperCollins.

* Grahame, Kenneth. *The Wind in the Willows*. Random House.

   Hastings, Selina. Reteller. *Sir Gawain and the Green Knight*. HarperCollins.

   Hoban, Russell. *The Mouse and His Child*. Scholastic.

   Jacques, Brian. *Mossflower*. Putnam.

*   _____. *Redwall*. Putnam.

* King-Smith, Dick. *A Mouse Called Wolf*. Random House.

* L'Engle, Madeleine. *A Wrinkle in Time*. Random House.

   Macaulay, David. *Castle*. Houghton Mifflin.

* O'Brien, Robert C. *Mrs. Frisby and the Rats of NIMH*. Simon & Schuster.

   Pye, Howard. *The Story of King Arthur and His Knights*. Dover.

* Rowling, J.K. *Harry Potter and the Chamber of Secrets*. Scholastic.

   _____. *Harry Potter and the Goblet of Fire*. Scholastic.

   _____. *Harry Potter and the Prisoner of Azkaban*. Scholastic.

*   _____. *Harry Potter and the Sorcerer's Stone*. Scholastic.

* Snicket, Lemony. *The Bad Beginning*. HarperCollins.

* Tolkien, J.R.R. *The Hobbit*. Random House.

* White, E.B. *Charlotte's Web*. HarperCollins.

*   _____. *Stuart Little*. HarperCollins.

Other Books by Kate DeCamillo

* *Because of Winn-Dixie*. Candlewick Press.

   The Magician's Elephant. Candlewick Press.

* *The Tiger Rising*. Candlewick Press.

* NOVEL-TIES Study Guides are available for these titles.

ANSWER KEY

Chapters 1-8

Vocabulary: 1. c 2. e 3. a 4. f 5. b 6. d; 1. rodents 2. ordeal 3. indulge 4. scurry 5. conform 6. siblings

Questions: 1. The mouse mother had a sense of great disappointment after the birth of her last baby. She vowed that she would not have any more mice babies because it was not worth the effort. She named him Despereaux because of all the sadness and despair that she felt. 2. All of the siblings and relatives were disappointed with Despereaux because he seemed odd in many ways. He was very small, was born with his eyes open, and he had obscenely large ears. He always seemed to be sick. Worst of all, he showed no interest in the things a mouse should show interest in, such as food. Instead he was interested in books, music, and light. 3. When Merlot took him into the library, Despereaux discovered books. Instead of eating them like other mice, Despereaux began to read the stories they contained. 4. Lester called a special meeting of the Mouse Council because he thought that Despereaux had done something that affected the safety and well-being of the entire mouse community. 5. Despereaux broke two basic and ancient mouse rules by allowing a human to see and touch him and by speaking to a human. He broke each rule because he was overcome by his love of music and his love of the princess. 6. King Philip felt that Princess Pea was breaking the rules of proper behavior because she was acting in a friendly way towards a mouse. He viewed this as wrong because mice are related to rats, and the king viewed all rats as his sworn enemies.

Chapters 9 – 15

Vocabulary: 1. c 2. a 3. d 4. b 5. c

Questions: 1. When first told that he had been called by the Mouse Council, Despereaux seemed very nonchalant and uninterested. It was not until he appeared before them that he realized the seriousness of his offense. 2. The Mouse Council accused Despereaux of sitting at the feet of the human king and allowing the human princess to touch him. He defended his actions by saying that he broke the rules for two reasons—because of music and because of love. 3. Despereaux refused to renounce his actions because by doing so he would be renouncing the princess, whom he loved. The mouse community was stunned and then infuriated with Despereaux's refusal to repent. 4. The threadmaster carried out the tradition of tying a red thread around Despereaux's neck to mark him for death in the dungeon. The threadmaster was the only mouse who wanted to know about the princess. He compared her to the princess of a fairy tale and told Despereaux that he loved her with a courtly love based on bravery, courtesy, honor, and devotion. 5. Despereaux could not forget the perfidy of his father and his brother because of the roles that they played in sending him to his death in the dungeon. 6. Despereaux comforted himself by telling himself a story about a knight in shining armor. 7. Gregory, the jailer who looked after the prisoners in the dungeon, offered to save Despereaux's life if Despereaux would tell him a story.

Chapters 16 – 18

Vocabulary: 1. e 2. f 3. a 4. b 5. d 6. c; 1. astute 2. obsession 3. despicable 4. solace 5. inordinate 6. domain

Questions: 1. The word *chiaroscuro* is a term used in art. It refers to the arrangement of light and dark and is used to create the illusion that a two-dimensional drawing or painting is three-dimensional. The character *Chiaroscuro* had elements of both light and darkness in his personality. He was a rat, which meant that he lived in the darkness of the dungeon and tortured prisoners sent there. But he also had discovered the beauty of light and longed for it. 2. Roscuro felt that the meaning of life was light; he was driven to go upstairs into the world of light. Botticelli felt that the meaning of life was darkness and to make others suffer. Botticelli advised Roscuro that causing the suffering of others was the way to invest life with meaning. 3. Botticelli felt there would soon be a prisoner that Roscuro could torture because the world is filled with evil, and evil guarantees the existence of prisoners. 4. Roscuro applied Botticelli's advice by winning the trust of the prisoner and then stealing his most precious possession, which was a red tablecloth. The result disappointed the rat. He realized that suffering was not the answer; instead it was going up into the light. 5. Roscuro wasn't shocked by the man's confession because he had heard Botticelli recite other even more terrible confessions that he had extracted from prisoners whom he had tortured. Roscuro believed men were capable of extraordinarily evil acts.

Chapters 19 – 23

Vocabulary: 1. d 2. f 3. a 4. c 5. b 6. e; 1. flung 2. dire 3. capacious 4. ornate 5. glaring 6. unsavory

Questions: 1.Roscuro, who had only experienced ugliness, darkness, and despair, was enchanted by all the things that glittered in the banquet hall. He was amazed by the beauty of the princess and

astounded by everyone's happiness. 2. Roscuro was struck by the ugliness of the word *rat* and all of the connotations associated with it. He realized that he did not like being a rat, the object of scorn and disgust. This sudden revelation caused him to loose his grip on the chandelier and fall into the queen's soup. The queen was so startled at seeing a rat in her soup that she died of shock. 3. Roscuro looked back over his shoulder because he remembered the prisoner's regret about not looking back when leaving his daughter. This backward glance broke Roscuro's heart because he saw how angry and disgusted the princess was with him. This made him realize that he would always have to live in darkness rather than in light. 4. Roscuro attempted to mend his broken heart by taking the queen's soupspoon so that he had something beautiful to take back into the darkness and by vowing that he would somehow have revenge on the princess and make her suffer for the way she looked at him. 5. King Philip was so heartbroken that he outlawed soup and all the instruments involved in the making of soup, such as kettles, bowls, and spoons. He also outlawed rats and ordered the death of every rat in the land. The banning of soup and the collection of all things used to make soup was successful, but it proved impossible to kill all the rats in the land because the rats in the dungeon could not be found. 6. All the instruments involved in the making and eating of soup were heaped in the dungeon after they had been confiscated by the King after the Queen's fatal encounter with soup.

Chapters 24 – 29
Vocabulary: 1. vicious 2. innumerable 3. clout 4. grim 5. scrupulously 6. bold
Questions: 1. It turns out that Mig was the daughter of the prisoner who revealed that he had sold his daughter for a red tablecloth, a hen, and a handful of cigarettes and never looked back. 2. Because Mig's master was cruel, he frequently gave her a clout to her ear, which caused her to have bad hearing. Because she couldn't hear, she couldn't understand what her master wanted her to do. Because she couldn't understand, she did more things wrong. Because she did things wrong, she would get more clouts to her ear, which meant she heard even less. 3. Light came into Mig's life the day she saw the royal family riding by. Seeing the princess made her hope to become a princess; it also made her hope to see the princess again. 4. Mig escaped when one of the king's men came by to collect soup-making paraphernalia. During the conversation, her owner let it slip that he owned his serving girl. When the king's servant heard this, he said that it was illegal to own anyone, and he carried Mig off to the castle. 5. Mig was allowed to visit Princess Pea to deliver a spool of red thread. Pea thought Mig's awkward curtsy was humorous. She appreciated the effort that Mig made even though it was unsuccessful. Pea was very sympathetic when she learned that Mig's mother had died. She only listened and didn't laugh or ridicule Mig's hope to become a princess. Pea's reactions showed that she was a kind, patient, and thoughtful person. 6. The spools of red thread have probably been stolen by the mice who use it as part of their punishment for nonconformist mice. 7. Louise laughed at the absurdity of Mig proclaiming that she would be a princess someday.

Chapters 30 – 33
Vocabulary: 1. oozing–the rest of the words are alike because they all describe something fearful or threatening 2. candle–the rest of the words are alike because they all name objects collected by order of the king in the story and stored in the dungeon 3. duchess–the rest of the words are alike because they all name jobs done by castle servants 4. napkin–the rest of the words are alike because they all name articles of clothing 5. diabolically–the rest of the words are alike because they all describe intense, positive feelings or emotions 6. aspiration–the rest of the words are alike because they all describe a great success
Questions: 1. In addition to her hearing problems, Mig was also a bit lazy and slow-witted, which meant that she couldn't understand what she was asked to do. As a consequence, she was sent to work in the kitchen and when that didn't work out, she was given the job of delivering Gregory's noonday meal to the dungeon. 2. Mig couldn't smell the stench of the dungeon because some of the clouts to her ears had landed on her nose and damaged her olfactory senses. She gave herself courage to go into the dungeon by talking and singing about her hope that someday she would be like the Princess Pea; when this happened she would be so glittery that no place in the world would seem dark to her. 3. Roscuro was delighted when he overheard Mig's conversation with Gregory in which she told him that someday she would be a princess. Roscuro saw Mig as an instrument to accomplish his revenge against Princess Pea. 4. Gregory helped Despereaux by hiding him in a napkin and slipping him on a tray for Mig to carry out of the dungeon. 5. Mig's conversation with Roscuro was different from those with others because she could actually hear what he was saying because of the pitch of his voice. Roscuro won her confidence by being polite, by knowing her name, and by telling her that he had a plan that could help her realize her dream of becoming a princess.

Chapters 34 – 39

Vocabulary: 1. slick–slippery   2. ominous–threatening   3. covert–secret or undercover   4. comeuppance–punishment that one deserves   5. dappled–marked with spots   6. empathetic–sharing of another's feeling

Questions: 1. Mig, although slow-witted, showed she had a good heart when she decided to let Despereaux escape. 2. Despereaux wept because he was in pain due to his severed tail and when, as revealed in his dream, he lost faith in the power of light over the dark: he wept for joy over the pleasure of being free and possibly being able to save Princess Pea from Roscuro's revenge. 3. Roscuro's plan for Princess Pea's "divine comeuppance" involved having Mig help him kidnap Pea in the middle of the night and hide her in the dungeon where she would never be found. He convinced Mig to join the plan by telling her that she and the princess would swap places; however, Roscuro never believed that that would happen. 4. Pea reacted with rage when she saw Roscuro because she recognized the soupspoon and knew that he was the rat that killed her mother by falling in the soup. 5. Cook and Louise were upset because Princess Pea was missing and no one could find her. They were also upset because they had learned of Gregory's death in the dungeon.

Chapters 40 – 46

Vocabulary: Across–1. inspiring   4. audible   7. empathetic   8. devious   9. despair   11. repent; Down–2. incredible   3. quest   5. uttered   6. maze   10. detect

Questions: 1. Upon seeing Despereaux, the members of the Mice Council were terrified because they thought they were seeing Despereaux's ghost. They refused to repent because they didn't believe that he was real. Only Despereaux's father asked for forgiveness for his perfidy. 2. Despereaux's father cried bittersweet tears because he believed that his son actually forgave him for cooperating with the Mouse Council to send him to his death. 3. King Philip did not believe Despereaux because he was a mouse, and the king viewed all rodents as liars. This made Despereaux realize that the task of saving the Princess was entirely up to him. 4. The threadmaster gave Despereaux the spool of red thread to guide him back through the dungeon and a needle to use as a sword. He also made Despereaux feel he had made a noble decision and that he was on a quest. He called Despereaux "a mouse among mice" because of his courage and his willingness to go back into the dungeon and risk his own life to rescue the princess. 5. Cook agreed not to kill Despereaux for being in her kitchen so long as he promised not to tell the king's men that she was breaking the law by making soup. She gave him a bowl of soup to drink before he went into the dungeon to make him feel stronger and more confident. 6. Despereaux felt overwhelmed by fear when he stood at the top of the stairs; he gained confidence by telling himself a story that was really about himself.

Chapters 47 – Coda

Vocabulary: 1. dire   2. thwarted   3. vengeful   4. atone   5. consigned   6. contemplate

Questions: 1. Botticelli offered to lead Despereaux to the princess because he believed that the best way to torture a prisoner was to give him what he most wanted and then take it away from him. 2. Roscuro revealed to Mig that she could never realize her hope of becoming a princess. He revealed to the princess that she would stay locked up in the dungeon forever and would never see light again. 3. Mig refused to chain up the princess because she finally realized that Roscuro did not care about her or what she wanted, but the princess did. 4. Roscuro wanted Despereaux to kill him because he realized his plan of bringing some light to the dungeon in the form of the princess would never work; he decided that it was better to die than to live without light. Pea intervened because she realized that only by offering Roscuro forgiveness and bringing him upstairs into the light would she find relief from the darkness in her heart that was caused by her hatred of the rat. 5. Despereaux was happy because he was able to be with the princess. Mig was happy because she was reunited with her father who finally showed her love. Roscuro was happy because he was able to come upstairs into the world of light. Cook was happy because the princess had been rescued and she was able to make soup again. The king was happy because the princess had been rescued and they were all together again. Pea was happy because the darkness and burden of hating Roscuro had been lifted from her heart.